Aslib Occasional Publication no.3

The Use of Bibliographic Records in Libraries

P. A. Thomas and H. East

Aslib

3 Belgrave Square, London SW1

SBN 85142 040 0

Price 26s
21s to members of Aslib

 PRINTED BY Unwin Brothers Limited
THE GRESHAM PRESS OLD WOKING SURREY ENGLAND

Produced by 'Uneoprint'

A member of the Staples Printing Group   (UCO4382)

Contents

Summary

We investigated the use of bibliographic records or forms in twelve libraries. It was necessary to examine the functions of each form in some detail and we were able to establish that, although the numbers and use of such forms varied widely in each of the libraries studied, those points in each procedure that need forms, and the information content necessary for a form to function effectively within a procedure, proved common to all libraries. We have therefore been able to demonstrate which elements of information, both bibliographic and administrative were present on actual forms used in the 12 libraries, and to suggest minimal information content requirements necessary to each stage of each procedure for a form to function effectively.

Introduction

Many library processes involve the clerical manipulation of records. Most of these records refer to a particular publication, and include a bibliographic description of it. To save labour, the intellectual work of making a bibliographic description of a publication should be done once only, and be recorded in such a way that it can be used in all subsequent library processing. Through the efforts of the British National Bibliography, there is now available a standard record on magnetic tape for publications passing through their hands. The library community faces the problem of making optimum use of this tape. Several libraries are undertaking practical investigations into this problem. In the study reported here, a theoretical approach is adopted.

Each library record includes not only a bibliographic description, but also local administrative data, and in processing both types of element must be combined. This paper reports on an analysis or procedures that has led to a classification of processes, applicable to all types of library, and a statement of what data elements (descriptive and administrative) are necessary for each activity within each process.

This analysis is the first step towards exploring an optimum record system. The schematic diagrams of this paper represent the unit activities that must be combined to form an integrated system of library processing. The next step is to consider the relationships between these units—inherent time sequence among the activities, and similarities of information content. It should be possible to link activities in a pattern that will minimise the need to recreate elements of information. This should provide an optimum configuration of procedures, that could be used in either a manual or machine system. A final step would be to take the tape record provided by the BNB, and to explore the ways in which it could be used in the optimum system, and the modifications that its use might entail.

The final result of a completed study would thus be to provide a generalised model for the use of the BNB tape record in integrated library processing. Only the first step is reported here.

B.C.Vickery

1

The Use of Bibliographic Records in Libraries

Background to the study

Current preoccupation with the use of data processing equipment in libraries has led us to a study of the present use of bibliographic records in library procedures. In particular, the possibility of having machine-readable records of bibliographic descriptions, prepared by central agencies such as the British National Bibliography and the Library of Congress, makes it appropriate to examine the elements of bibliographic description, their present uses, and their possible uses if freed from traditional concepts and practice. There are at least two good reasons for doing this: first, in the interests of efficiency, if information not relevant to a particular procedure is nevertheless processed in that procedure it is time-consuming and pointless; second, if the generalized 'communication format' of the centrally produced machine-readable records is to be used effectively by individual libraries, the subsets of elements required for each process must be carefully defined. Information once recorded could then be manipulated by machine and used for other purposes without wasteful duplication of effort.

A bibliographic record is made up of elements of description (e.g. author, title, collation). The traditional bibliographic record is the catalogue entry, whose component elements have been a focus of attention and discussion from the first compilation of a set of catalogue rules to the current concern with the computer generation and manipulation of such entries. Attention has centred on the identification, description and exhaustive listing of elements that can be used in this traditional record (references 1, 2, 3). Little has been done to examine systematically all the bibliographical records necessary to the organization of library systems. Apart from the standard descriptive elements, each library has to process local administrative information (e.g. dates, order numbers, accession numbers). Records used in a particular procedure will usually combine both types of element.

A much clearer understanding of what records are necessary in the organization of library systems, their value and the part they play, is a prerequisite for the beneficial application of new techniques. It is also a valuable aid in the evaluation of present situations. It is possible that the BNB/MARC communication record may be used to generate bibliographic records for any procedure which needs them, although this assumes that the elements of bibliographic description used in other library procedures are sub-sets of those traditionally employed by catalogue production. To know which elements are needed for the efficient functioning of library operations, we need to identify all bibliographic records used in libraries and analyse their use within each procedure.

Aims and method of procedure

Vickery (reference 1) has defined the four purposes of bibliographic elements as follows:

(a) collectively, the elements in a record describe and identify a bibliographic item

(b) each element can in principle serve as a retrieval key by which records that show a common characteristic can be selected

(c) the symbolic forms in which each element is recorded may facilitate clerical arrangement of records into an ordered sequence

(d) one element can indicate the location where the item itself is stored

We have so far concentrated on the first of these purposes, and attempted to identify and investigate the use of elements of information, both those of a purely bibliographic and those of a local nature, in records presently maintained and used in libraries. Our project aimed to discover:

(a) what kinds of bibliographic records are currently made

(b) what descriptive elements go into each kind of record

(c) what purposes are served by these bibliographic records

(d) what purposes are served by each element in each record

(e) and therefore, which set of elements would form an 'optimal' bibliographic record.

We postulated that a systematic way of acquiring information about essential bibliographic descriptions in libraries was to trace and collect their manifestations as 'forms'. Practically every library operation involves the use of forms, although few libraries have consciously designed sets of forms. Single forms have more often evolved for specific procedures or activities, and then been formalized. We have taken the very broad definition that a form, for the purposes of our investigation, is any document containing individual identifications of bibliographic items expressed by means of elements of bibliographic description. Examples of such forms are order form, book card, accessions register, and the writing on the flyleaf of a book for use in photocharging.

In this study we have ignored purely administrative records which do not contain elements of bibliographic description, that is those forms concerned primarily with personnel, financial, or statistical information. We have, however, noted local elements of information where they occurred in the same context as, and were used in conjunction with, bibliographic information. For example, a reservation record may contain author and title (bibliographic information) and date of application with user's name and address (local information).

We have made an intensive study of the records used in three libraries in each of the following groups:

1. Public libraries (one London borough, one municipal, one county)

2. University libraries (one ancient, one modern, one redbrick)

3. Non-commercial special libraries (one government, 2 learned societies)

4. Commercial and industrial special libraries.

This mix of libraries is not only varied in the scope of operations, but also considerably in size, the largest having a stock of over two million volumes, the smallest a few hundred. We have followed the view expressed by Goldstein (reference 4) and Levi-Strauss (reference 5), that limiting oneself to a thorough study of a small number of cases is more valuable in permitting the formulation of final judgements, than studying many cases in a superficial and in the end ineffective way.

About a week on average was spent at each of the libraries under study in collecting forms and recording descriptions of the procedures that involved them. Enumerating the forms of a library is by no means a straightforward procedure. Our findings were well in line with those of Knox (reference 6), who has concerned himself with the design and control of forms in the office situation and says

'it is not unusual for a company to find anywhere from fifty to an hundred per cent more forms than anyone thought it had'. Estimates by the library staff of 'about a dozen' could precede the discovery of eighty or more discrete information-carrying documents. We talked to the librarian of each library and identified the various departments, and then interviewed each department head to get an outline of his department's activities, and its position within the organization's structure. The activities were then examined in more detail. We collected an example of each form involved and charted its use by talking to the members of staff responsible. Information concerning the files created, updated or examined in the course of the procedure was also noted.

We are grateful for the help and cooperation of all the people we met, which was particularly noticeable when we carefully explained that we were not from any O & M department, and had indeed some knowledge and personal experience of library work. The whole subject of forms control and design, although a rather neglected field in the library situation, is one which evokes a surprising degree of interest and enthusiasm.

Preliminary analysis

Initially we studied our descriptions of the basic procedures of the libraries we had visited. In our sample, which contained libraries that differed widely in size, age, stock, user population, and mission of the parent organization, we found a great deal of similarity in the basic procedures related to acquiring, maintaining and providing access to library materials. Moreover, there is a corresponding relationship between the functions fulfilled within these procedures by the bibliographic records involved.

There are, of course, wide differences in form generation and usage from library to library. The most apparent differences concern number and format and are not primarily connected with functions fulfilled by the forms, nor with the size and type of library, but arise from apparently arbitrary variations in the use of these records throughout each system. In some libraries one form fulfils a number of functions and is used in connection with more than one procedure, being moved from department to department or file to file. In others, multiple copies of a particular form are generated at one procedural point and the copies distributed to perform a number of functions. Other libraries use different forms for each function, and bibliographic information commonly required for interconnected procedures is regenerated as and when required.

Other differences arise for the most part from a shift of emphasis in service to the library user, from the supply of a book or document to that of informa-

tion; and from specialized local activities such as thesis collection in universities, current awareness services of special libraries, and educational responsibilities of public libraries. These factors will more closely concern a later stage of the project, the use of locally prepared bibliographic tools both by the user alone and the user in association with a librarian.

The similarity lies in the functions these forms fulfil; that is, libraries of all types need bibliographic records, at least in the common core activities identified, for the same functions in connection with the same activities.

The definition, at a fundamental level, of what are the functions of a particular form, is necessary if one hopes to isolate an optimum set of bibliographic elements for library systems. It is not enough to know what, traditionally, are the elements used in following a particular procedure. We must examine what part is played by each element, first to justify its inclusion, and second to determine the form in which it should be available. We have here particularly concerned ourselves with the first of these requirements, and have endeavoured to establish the essential information content of a record necessary to its effective use within a procedure.

In order to demonstrate our observations on the use of bibliographic records in the framework of the library system, we have evolved an hierarchical model of functional levels (see next page).

We have, as explained, concerned ourselves with the operational rather than the administrative side of the system. It has been useful to categorise the basic work of a library as the sub-systems Acquisition, Processing, Use and Maintenance. (We have limited our detailed study to monographic material.) At the next level of systems organization we have defined the eighteen procedures which make up these sub-systems. The procedures have been given the following names:

Subsystem	Procedure
Acquisition	select
	order
	receive
Processing	accession
	classify
	catalogue
	label
	shelve
Use	locate
	list
	lend
	reserve
	recall
	inter-library loans (borrow and return)
	photocopy
Maintenance	bind
	replace
	discard

3

Functional Levels in a Library System

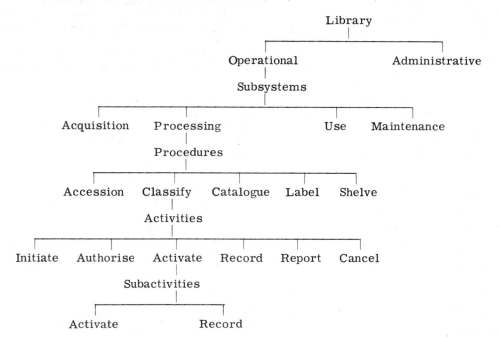

These procedures are characteristic of libraries of all types and involve the use of forms containing bibliographic information.

We find that within these procedures it is possible to distinguish six activities, whose collective function is the accomplishment of that procedure. A form functions within the system according to those activities with which it is linked. It must be emphasised that a particular form may, and often does, have several functions (interpreted within the context of these activities), and may be used in a number of different procedures. The following is an attempt at a definition of the functions of forms within the activities of each procedure:

1. initiate — this activity occurs when something makes it apparent that a procedure should be commenced. It can be through a form from a previous procedure, it can be a form from outside the library, e.g. publisher's catalogue, BNB or a Regional loans form, it can be the book itself, or a telephone call from a library user.

2. authorise — this activity occurs when the decision to carry out a certain procedure must be approved before any further action is taken. This is usually shown by the signing of a form.

3. activate — the activity that implements a procedure known to be necessary and approved. It is usually implemented by means of a form. We have also used the term to include the idea of reactivation or follow-up of a procedure, e.g. letters sent to suppliers on non-arrival, as well as the original order, activate the ordering procedure.

4. record — the function fulfilled by a form that states or records what action has been taken.

5. report — the activity of notifying someone, library staff or user, that an action has been taken.

6. cancel — the activity of stopping a procedure, in particular the aspect of revoking or undoing an action, e.g. un-issuing a book is the cancellation of the lending procedure.

Not all activities are necessary to each procedure and some of them may be carried out by forms, some by word of mouth or by using material (such as publishers' catalogues) generated outside the library system; but this list has been found to cover all cases of form usage studied.

As an example, a given form can initiate and authorise the selection procedure; initiate and in some cases activate the ordering procedure, record receipt and finally be used as a permanent record in the accession procedure. In this particular example, the multi-function form is not only used in several procedures, but also passes from one sub-system to another.

The six functions we have identified are at a more basic level than that usually referred to in the library context, where the function of a form is more loosely tied to the procedural level e.g. 'order' forms, 'accession' registers. The lowest identifiable level of our model, which we have called subactivities, emphasises the two immediate and essential functions of a form when used as an operational tool. These are the activating and, when filed, the recording of one of the six possible activities involved in a procedure. While these two subactivities are not self-sufficient, they are identifiable components of the main activity. Previous authors have not found it necessary to distinguish between these subactivities, let alone name them. We have found, however, that the real use of a form, whatever procedures it is linked with, needs to be examined in this amount of detail before the reasons for inclusion or exclusion of elements of information can be fully justified.

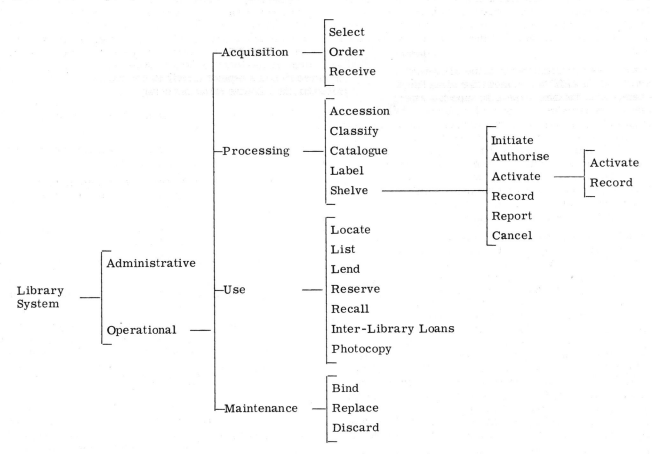

Presentation of results

We have noted all elements of information used, whether elements of bibliographic description concerned with the identity of a particular bibliographic item, or procedure-directed elements such as date of receipt and signature of authorisation (those elements detailed as 'local' by Curran and Avram in reference 2). This type of information is linked with a particular bibliographic item, although describing operations on the item and not the item itself, and is of vital importance in considering the functions of each form and the use made of the elements of bibliographic description. The two types of information are interdependent and a knowledge of their interaction is necessary in considering any possible application of centrally generated bibliographic information.

There does not seem to be any standard set of data available on which to base a decision concerning which set of activities or procedures a particular form is to be linked with. No one library assigned a form to the same combination of activities and procedures.

We have analysed forms used to activate or record each activity within a procedure, and drawn schematic diagrams showing which elements of description are present at each stage. The resulting diagrams show a consensus of opinion on which elements should be included, exemplified by forms used in the 12 libraries studied. Each of these diagrams therefore gives a maximal entry; that is, no further elements were found necessary in any of the 12 libraries for the form to fulfil its function.

When studying the use of the form at each functional level there are a number of related factors to be

taken into consideration. These are, briefly, who does what to both elements and form, and for whom. That is, elements of information (bibliographical and non-bibliographical) are entered on the form, or checked (that is, read and acted on) by and for one or more of the following groups of people:

1. Library staff

2. Library users

3. Library suppliers
    (booksellers and binders)

The form itself can be circulated or passed from one person/group of people to another in order to fulfil its function. This affects not only the information content but also the presentation of the content. At various stages the form will be filed. These files may be of any physical kind, from card catalogues to a few pieces of paper clipped together, and can be permanent or temporary and designed for use by members of more than one group. Forms can also be discarded. Even taking all these factors into account, in many cases it appears that more information is included than is actually needed. The main reason for this, of course, is that one form fulfils a number of functions, as explained above, and presumably the information apparently superfluous at one stage is thought to be necessary to another.

All the libraries examined had forms functioning in the identified manner within the same procedures, but the number, format and information content differed because of the variance in usage. No two libraries will necessarily use any one form in the same combination of procedures. In some libraries the emphasis is on movement of a form from department to department and file to file, in others on the production and distribution of multiple copies of a form. There does not at present appear to be an innate reason for using a form in a particular way, nor for tying it to a particular additional set of procedures.

If we consider the possible use of records generated from the BNB/MARC tapes, knowledge of two things is necessary. The time-base is an important aspect when linking procedures through use of forms in this way, and the necessary information content for each activity involved in the procedure/s must be effectively determined. Our listing of procedures and activities has an inherent time sequence; apart from this, other determining factors must be the availability of BNB/MARC material and local constraints. We have concentrated on the information content needs of each activity and procedure.

This knowledge is also essential to a non-machine based consideration of a library system. Our method of investigation has close affinities with the structural methods detailed in the work of Levi-Strauss and other writers, and has revealed itself as a technique adaptable for looking at libraries and one that could well be developed in connection with other matters than forms. Concentrating on the bibliographic context, as we have, has shown that this embraces the main range of technical or professional work in libraries. In any evaluation of an existing system, and any work on improving or redesigning certain areas of it, this knowledge is most valuable. The "form", as in our definition is the most used, and most powerful of operational tools, and a close understanding of its content and function is essential.

It seems that as the level of function we have identified is common not only to the procedures listed, but to their operation in libraries of different types, then this information should be helpful in deciding which elements constitute an optimal record. All functions of forms derived from it should be considered. Therefore, having used the form as the vehicle for collecting our information, we now present our analysis of the functioning of elements of information related to the activities and procedures for which they are needed, and divorce them from their manifestations on individual forms. We show this in the guise of schematic diagrams, for ease in referring and comparing the lists of elements, and developed from an idea in Cox and Grose (reference 7).

The schematic diagrams

We present two schematic diagrams for each of our eighteen procedures, except cataloguing which will be treated separately. The first of each pair is a 'consensus' diagram showing all elements of information present on all the forms used in the procedure in the libraries studied. Not all elements were needed for each of the activities in the procedure and if their presence seems surprising, it may be assumed to be connected with other activities and procedures the form was incidentally connected with. Each of these diagrams therefore, gives a *maximal* entry; that is, no further elements were found necessary in any of the twelve libraries for the form to function in the named procedure. We have allocated numbers to each element in a procedure according to which of the six activities within the procedure it was present.

The strings of element boxes have an underlying classificatory base, being grouped roughly according to type of information conveyed, as in the first diagram. This details all elements of information with which we are concerned. Those elements which are underlined are present in the BNB/MARC communication record. Interpretation of the exact significance of the named elements depends largely on context. In particular, the following variations occur:

Volume — volume number *or* number of volumes

Vendor — bookseller *or* binder, interpret as booksupplier

No. copies — may also mean copy number where accession number is not used to differentiate

Library — name of main library, branch library, other library

User — covers name *or* name and address of user

Signature — may refer to library staff *or* library user

Abstract — includes brief annotations as to contents or particular importance of item

Note: B. Source stands for bibliographic source of original reference.

Those bibliographical items in the first two strings, such as an additional authors, sub-title and series note, may be assumed to occur in the procedure indicated only when appropriate; that is when present in original bibliographical item and necessary to its individual identification. We have detailed them in the optimal presentations only for the listing procedure, where their presense is obligatory.

The second of each pair of diagrams show our suggestions for the information content of *optimal* records for each procedure. We have concentrated on the information requirements appropriate to each activity rather than visualising individual forms, and therefore include here, particularly at the initiation stage of some procedures, vital information presented by the book itself. Each element is required for that activity with which it is numbered, for the full procedure the total elements used summarise the necessary configuration. From this we could build up (or extract from the BNB/MARC record) an optimal record for any desired combination of activities and procedures, so giving a functional basis to the inclusion or exclusion of elements of information.

The design and control of forms for use in library procedures is not central to our present project; neither is the consideration of possible advantageous standardisation, although the basic similarity of the requirements of the libraries we visited is most striking, and work along both these lines could well prove worth developing. The method of analysis we have used promises possible development as a technique in a non-forms-directed investigation of procedures. We intend to explore this, with particular emphasis on the design of a procedural model of a library system.

The Schematic Diagrams

The subscripts shown in the element boxes indicate the presence of an element in the six activities, as follows:

Subscript	Activity
1	Initiate
2	Authorise
3	Activate
4	Record
5	Report
6	Cancel

The first of each diagrams is the consensus one, and the second the optimal one.

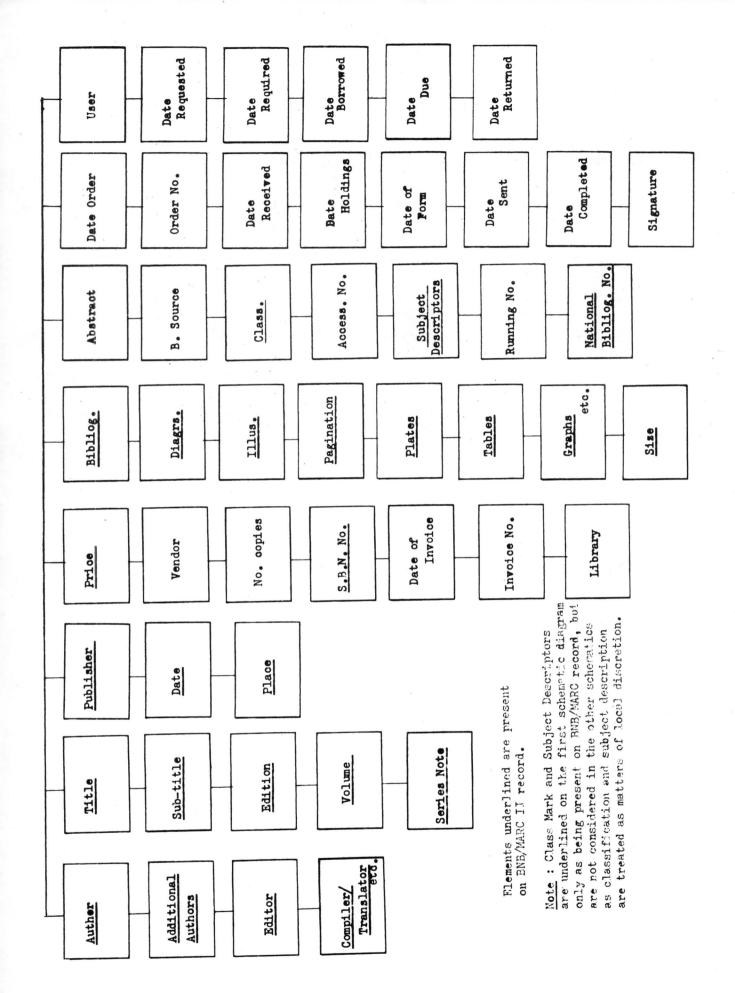

Elements underlined are present on BNB/MARC II record.

Note : Class Mark and Subject Descriptors are underlined on the first schematic diagram only as being present on BNB/MARC record, but are not considered in the other schematics as classification and subject description are treated as matters of local discretion.

Acquisition: Select.

The medium which can initiate this procedure may be generated either within or outside the library system. It can be publicity material or trade lists from a publishing firm, or hand-written suggestions from library users on library-supplied stationery, or can result from stock-editing work by library staff. The information given will vary according to its source, and range from the full bibliographic descriptions supplied by some reputable publishing houses to the briefest of details hopefully remembered by a library user. All these records are directed towards members of the library staff, and in the case of user-recommendations can involve appreciable effort in bibliographical checking.

The form itself can be circulated, is subject to emendation and annotation, and may be filed at various stages of its life, e.g. 'awaiting consideration; to be ordered; rejected suggestions'. The most appropriate filing key for all of these is the author's name.

Authorisation by senior staff is usually required and indicated by the addition of the appropriated signature. Activation may be carried out by the same form as that which initiated and/or authorised selection, or may need a new one. Recording decision and action on the procedure is, as in most procedures, accomplished by filing a copy of the form used in one of the previous activities, and can well be annotated according to later ones in the same, or a later procedure.

Some libraries report to, or notify, the user if an item suggested is to be ordered, or may query bibliographical details with him if those given are insufficient for identification. In these cases, besides minimal descriptive elements, details on library and user are needed. It is, however, more usual for a library to notify a user only when the required item is to hand and has been processed ready for loan. Cancellation at the selection stage is rare, but can be accomplished by annotation of existing forms, particularly of that used for recording action taken.

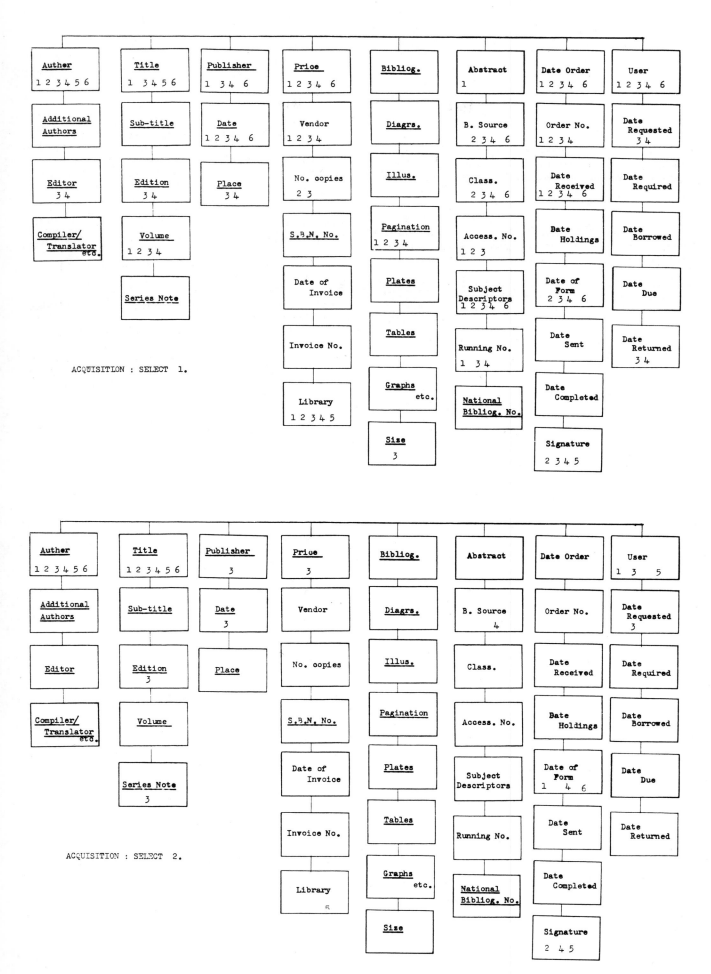

ACQUISITION : SELECT 1.

ACQUISITION : SELECT 2.

Acquisition: Order

The medium which initiates the ordering procedure may be a form produced in the library at the previous selection stage, marked copies of published lists or *BNB*. It may be a suggestion card from a library user. The information supplied will vary according to its source. We would suggest those elements marked with the subscript 1 on the relevant diagram as the basic elements of information required to initiate this procedure.

Authorisation of this procedure may take place before or after activation, indeed authorisation at the selection stage is often accounted sufficient for the ordering procedure also. Besides minimum identifying bibliographic elements, the only other items of information necessary are signature and date of action (which latter we have classed with date of form for convenience).

The activation of the ordering procedure involves that form usually referred to as an 'order form'. Here, the librarian is supplying information to the book-seller on items required. In addition to ele-ments of bibliographic description there-fore, information referring to the transaction itself is required; vendor's name, number and date of order, library requesting the books-all these items we mark with the subscript 3 on the diagrams. The order form, or a copy of it, is then sent to the bookseller.

Recording the ordering procedure is usually accomplished by filing a copy of the 'order form' itself. No further information is necessary at this stage. The file, of course, is often involved in the later procedure of receipt when the forms are annotated as necessary, but this does not concern us here. Reporting to, or notifying, the user if an item suggested by him is on order, again involves minimal descriptive elements, and those concerning library and user.

To cancel an item already ordered, it is necessary to give the supplier enough information to identify both the bibliographic item and the original order details, and often involves the use of a new form. It may well be necessary to authorise and date the cancellation, and the recording of the original order must also be annotated with action and date.

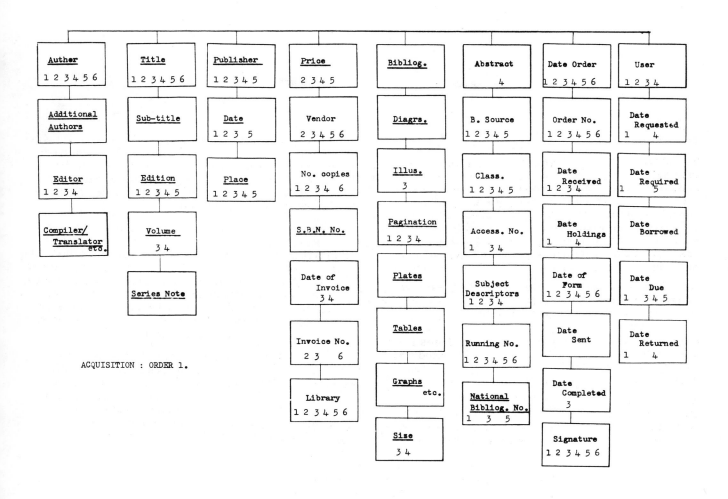

ACQUISITION : ORDER 1.

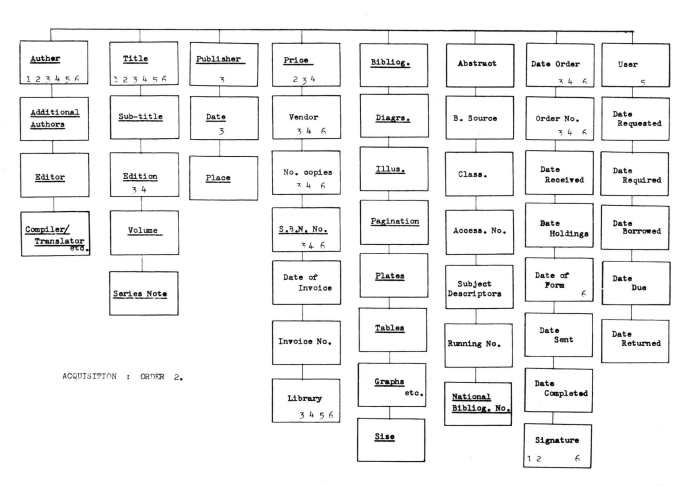

ACQUISITION : ORDER 2.

Acquisition: Receive

This procedure is most often accomplished by the annotation of a previous record, one involved in the ordering process. Indeed, the three procedures in the acquisition sub-system can usefully be grouped together and dealt with by using the same form, or set of forms. Full bibliographical details are necessary for the identification of the item involved, plus the administrative information on the particular transaction, as in the original ordering.

The only two activities we have detailed as applicable to this procedure are those of recording and reporting action taken (that is, the receipt). The recording is strictly for library staff use, although for our purposes this includes internal accounts and auditing staff whether affiliated with the parent organisation or officially appointed for overlooking financial matters. The reporting as well is necessary mainly for these reasons, but can also refer to user notification if this is dealt with at this stage.

There is a strong relationship between these three procedures, as noted above, and an in-built time sequence. The possibility of exploiting this by linking the activities and forms involved has been mentioned. The main difficulties concern the varying amount of information supplied by the different sources in the selection procedure, and the availability of enough of this information in a standard format at a sufficiently early date to allow confidence in organising the procedures in this way.

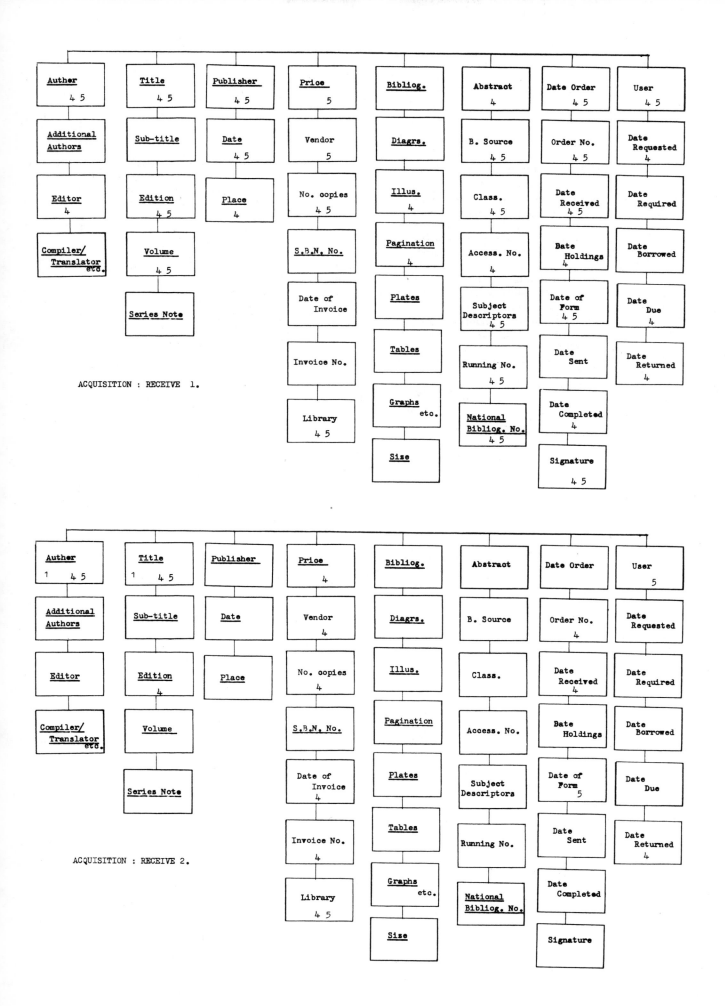

Auther 45	Title 45	Publisher 45	Price 5	Bibliog.	Abstract 4	Date Order 45	User 45
Additional Authors	Sub-title	Date 45	Vendor 5	Diagrs.	B. Source 45	Order No. 45	Date Requested 4
Editor 4	Edition 45	Place 4	No. copies 45	Illus. 4	Class. 45	Date Received 45	Date Required
Compiler/ Translator etc.	Volume 45		S.B.N. No.	Pagination 4	Access. No. 4	Bate Holdings 4	Date Borrowed
	Series Note		Date of Invoice	Plates	Subject Descriptors 45	Date of Form 45	Date Due 4
			Invoice No.	Tables	Running No. 45	Date Sent	Date Returned 4
			Library 45	Graphs etc.	National Bibliog. No. 45	Date Completed 4	
				Size		Signature 45	

ACQUISITION : RECEIVE 1.

Auther 1 45	Title 1 45	Publisher	Price 4	Bibliog.	Abstract	Date Order	User 5
Additional Authors	Sub-title	Date	Vendor 4	Diagrs.	B. Source	Order No. 4	Date Requested
Editor	Edition 4	Place	No. copies 4	Illus.	Class.	Date Received 4	Date Required
Compiler/ Translator etc.	Volume		S.B.N. No.	Pagination	Access. No.	Bate Holdings	Date Borrowed
	Series Note		Date of Invoice 4	Plates	Subject Descriptors	Date of Form 5	Date Due
			Invoice No. 4	Tables	Running No.	Date Sent	Date Returned 4
			Library 45	Graphs etc.	National Bibliog. No.	Date Completed	
				Size		Signature	

ACQUISITION : RECEIVE 2.

Processing: Accession

Accessioning is usually the first of the technical processes a book is subjected to once it is received in the library. Although there is a move to abolish the accessions register in many libraries now, there is a disinclination to forget the whole idea, and it can linger on in the continuing allocation of accession numbers without the recording of these in a register. It is generally agreed that it is useful to have an individual number for each book for identification and inventorial functions. It is, of course, particularly necessary in the Brown charging system, and it has been found easier and quicker to use a numerical filing key as opposed to an alphabetical one. This is also borne out by the running numbers given to a fair proportion of the forms investigated.

The accession number is generated by and for library staff on the most part, although library suppliers are sometimes provided with a block of accession numbers when they are involved in the processing of books for the library, and library users can be asked to quote the accession number when renewing loans by telephone or postcard.

Initiation of this procedure is usually triggered by the appearance of the book/s on the desk of the number of staff responsible for the accessioning routine. This supplies the bibliographic details. Activation is through the allocation of an accession number, which number can then stand as a shorthand identification of the book implying the usual bibliographic description. Recording is done by re-stating the bibliographic details in some kind of accessions register.

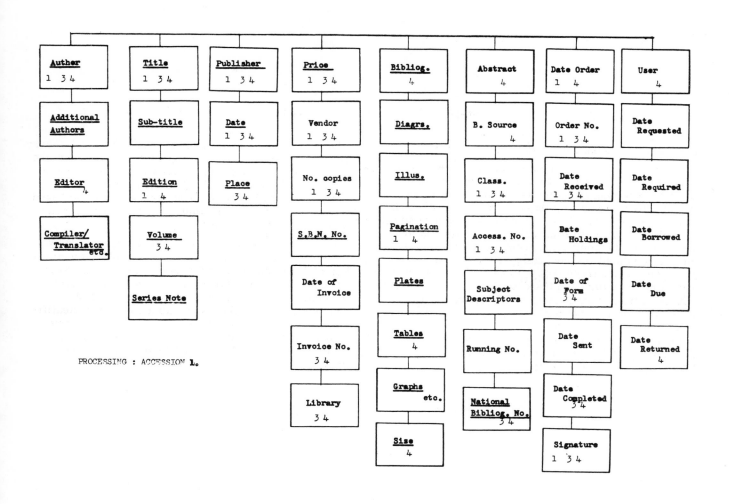

Auther 1 3 4	Title 1 3 4	Publisher 1 3 4	Price 1 3 4	Bibliog. 4	Abstract 4	Date Order 1 4	User 4
Additional Authors	Sub-title	Date 1 3 4	Vendor 1 3 4	Diagrs.	B. Source 4	Order No. 1 3 4	Date Requested
Editor 4	Edition 1 4	Place 3 4	No. copies 1 3 4	Illus.	Class. 1 3 4	Date Received 1 3 4	Date Required
Compiler/ Translator etc.	Volume 3 4		S.B.N. No.	Pagination 1 4	Access. No. 1 3 4	Bate Holdings	Date Borrowed
	Series Note		Date of Invoice	Plates	Subject Descriptors	Date of Form 3 4	Date Due
			Invoice No. 3 4	Tables 4	Running No.	Date Sent	Date Returned 4
			Library 3 4	Graphs etc.	National Bibliog. No. 3 4	Date Completed 3 4	
				Size 4		Signature 1 3 4	

PROCESSING : ACCESSION 1.

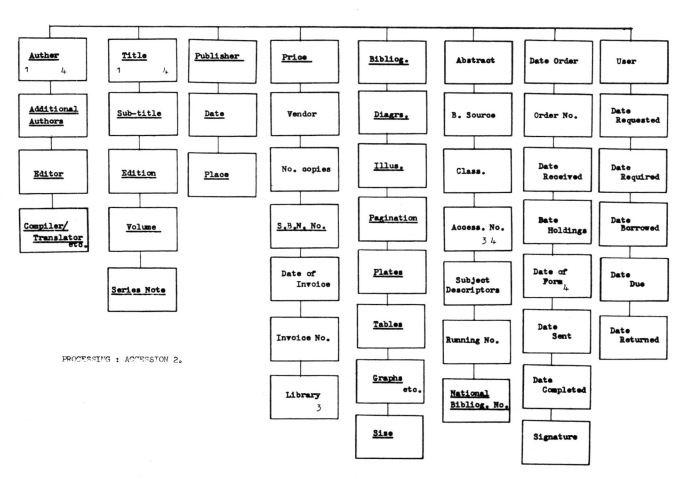

Auther 1 4	Title 1 4	Publisher	Price	Bibliog.	Abstract	Date Order	User
Additional Authors	Sub-title	Date	Vendor	Diagrs.	B. Source	Order No.	Date Requested
Editor	Edition	Place	No. copies	Illus.	Class.	Date Received	Date Required
Compiler/ Translator etc.	Volume		S.B.N. No.	Pagination	Access. No. 3 4	Bate Holdings	Date Borrowed
	Series Note		Date of Invoice	Plates	Subject Descriptors	Date of Form 4	Date Due
			Invoice No.	Tables	Running No.	Date Sent	Date Returned
			Library 3	Graphs etc.	National Bibliog. No.	Date Completed	
				Size		Signature	

PROCESSING : ACCESSION 2.

Processing: Classify

This procedure is again initiated by the books themselves, and activation and recording are accomplished
by the allocation of a class mark to each book. Recording of this procedure is also signified by the addition
of the class mark to such relevant records as the
catalogue entry, author and/or classified, and through
the subsequent labelling procedure.

Cancellation may be defined in this context as re-
classification.

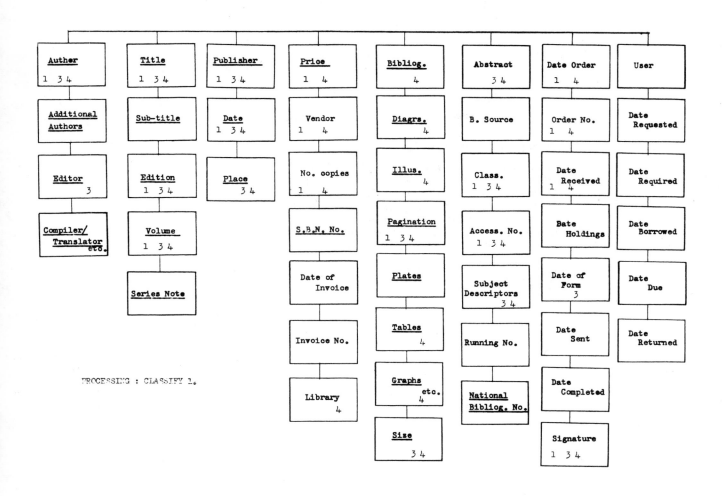

PROCESSING : CLASSIFY 1.

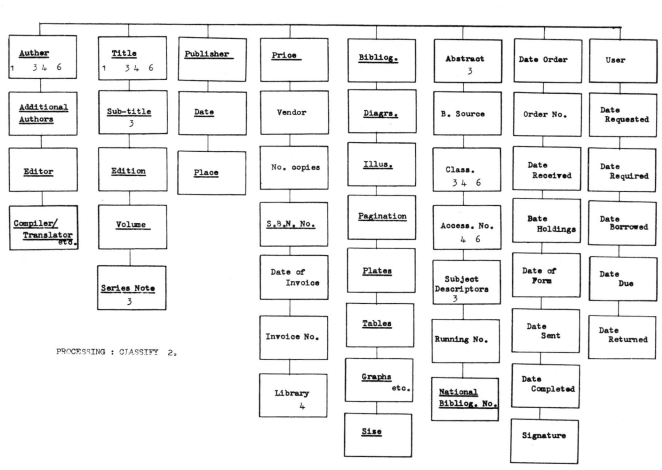

PROCESSING : CLASSIFY 2.

19

Processing: Label

Similarly initiated and activated to the above, and again dealt with by library staff, the results of this procedure are directed to both staff and users. This procedure is almost limited in effect to a recording activity of both the accession and classification procedures, but has been considered separately because of its position in the functional levels, and its importance in the processing sub-system of each library. Cancellation would be defined as re-labelling if and when necessary.

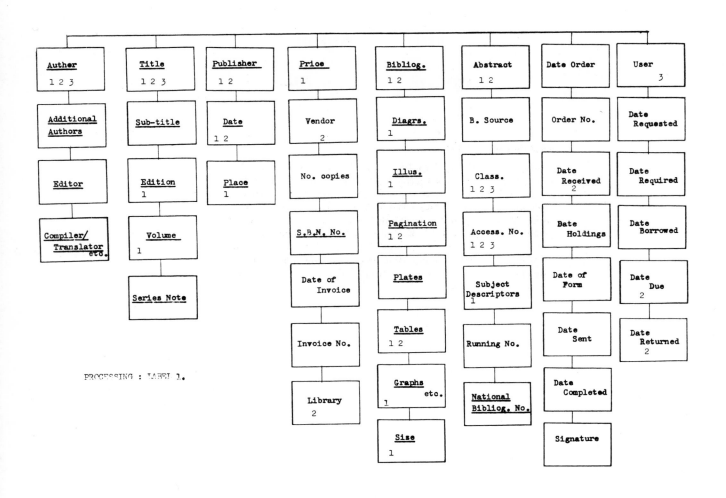

PROCESSING : LABEL 1.

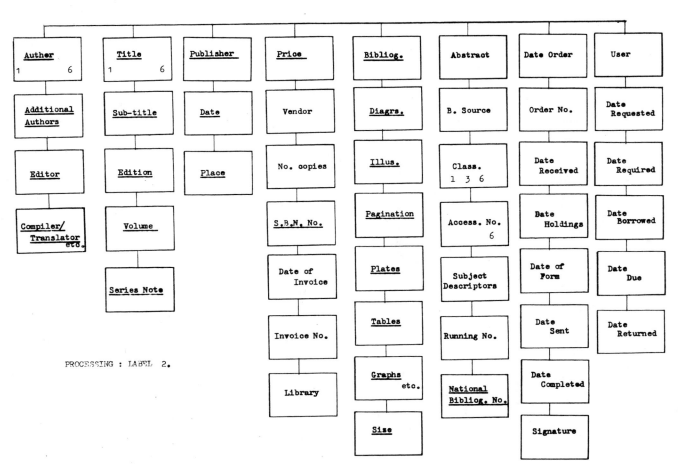

PROCESSING : LABEL 2.

Processing: Shelve

Shelving is initiated by the book itself, and activated
and recorded by the book, or rather the labelling on
the spine of the book. Therefore, forms (or labels in
this case) are actually involved only in the last two
activities. A kind of cancellation of the action may be
defined as the re-arrangement of books already
shelved, and involves the use of the same information.
The work is done by library staff for both staff and
users.

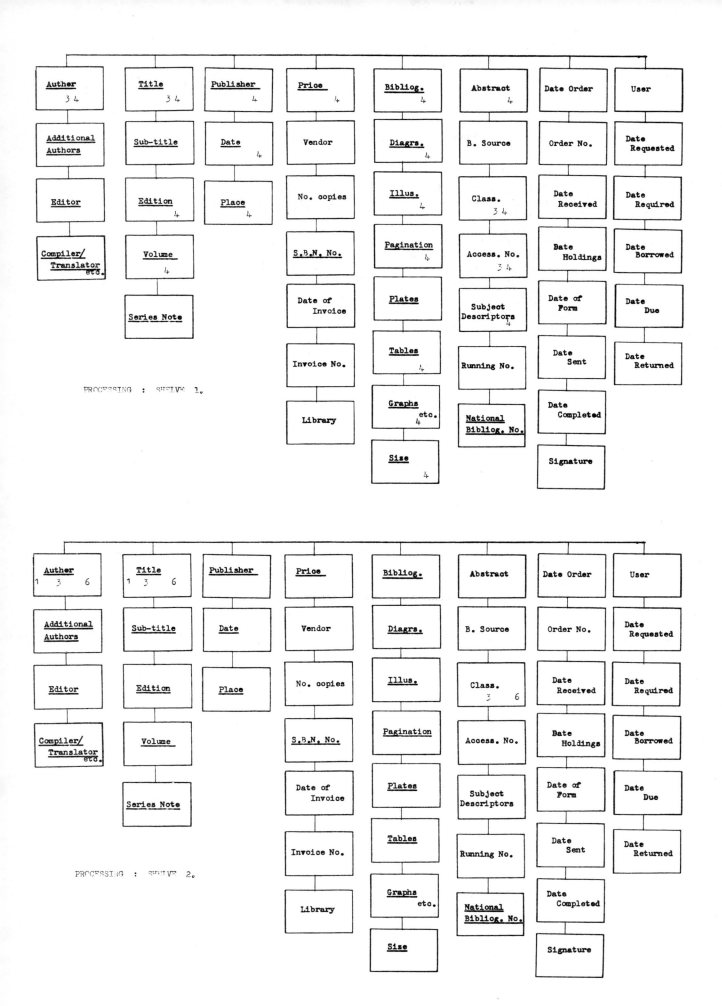

PROCESSING : SHELVE 1.

PROCESSING : SHELVE 2.

Use: Locate

The initiation of this procedure may be by means of a telephone enquiry, conversation with library user, or letter. The amount of detail will depend on the user, or member of staff involved if the enquiry is an internal one. We would say that before proceeding to the next activity, author, title, user and/or subject and user information must be obtained.

Activation and recording may be done by using a form. The person receiving the original request may not be the one who deals with an enquiry, and telephone calls are often noted down on scrap paper if no other form is provided. Other elements of possible importance for these two activities are accession number, and date due if required item is already on loan.

There is no standard way of recording this procedure, and some libraries do not keep any records of past enquiries, apart from noting one or two unusual ones in their annual reports. Numbers of enquiries received and dealt with can give some indication of library use, although it is not so helpful to then try to work out how much staff time was involved in such work. It has been argued that having answered one enquiry in a subject field, it is useful and time-saving to record findings for possible future use, but this involves the maintenance of such records and a happy trust in expecting similar enquiries to occur. It can be demonstrated as a useful practice in a particular local situation, but the time and effort in keeping such records probably outweighs benefits.

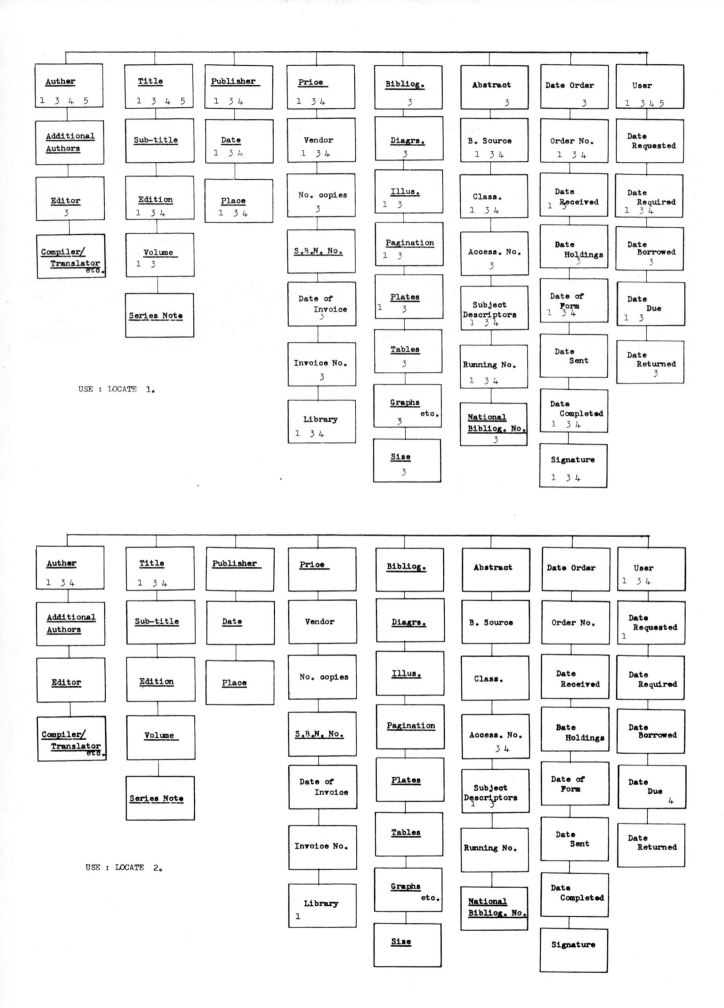

Diagram 1 (top)

Auther 1 3 4 5	Title 1 3 4 5	Publisher 1 3 4	Price 1 3 4	Bibliog. 3	Abstract 3	Date Order 3	User 1 3 4 5
Additional Authors	Sub-title	Date 1 3 4	Vendor 1 3 4	Diagrs. 3	B. Source 1 3 4	Order No. 1 3 4	Date Requested
Editor 3	Edition 1 3 4	Place 1 3 4	No. copies 3	Illus. 1 3	Class. 1 3 4	Date Received 1 3	Date Required 1 3 4
Compiler/ Translator etc.	Volume 1 3		S.B.N. No.	Pagination 1 3	Access. No. 3	Bate Holdings 3	Date Borrowed 3
	Series Note		Date of Invoice 3	Plates 1 3	Subject Descriptors 1 3 4	Date of Form 1 3 4	Date Due 1 3
			Invoice No. 3	Tables 3	Running No. 1 3 4	Date Sent	Date Returned 3
			Library 1 3 4	Graphs etc. 3	National Bibliog. No. 3	Date Completed 1 3 4	
				Size 3		Signature 1 3 4	

USE : LOCATE 1.

Diagram 2 (bottom)

Auther 1 3 4	Title 1 3 4	Publisher	Price	Bibliog.	Abstract	Date Order	User 1 3 4
Additional Authors	Sub-title	Date	Vendor	Diagrs.	B. Source	Order No.	Date Requested 1
Editor	Edition	Place	No. copies	Illus.	Class.	Date Received	Date Required
Compiler/ Translator etc.	Volume		S.B.N. No.	Pagination	Access. No. 3 4	Bate Holdings	Date Borrowed
	Series Note		Date of Invoice	Plates	Subject Descriptors 1 3	Date of Form	Date Due 4
			Invoice No.	Tables	Running No.	Date Sent	Date Returned
			Library 1	Graphs etc.	National Bibliog. No.	Date Completed	
				Size		Signature	

USE : LOCATE 2.

Use: List

This procedure can be initiated by forms involved
in any of the preceding ones, or indeed by the books
themselves. Degree of information at this stage will
of course depend on forms or books involved. Activation is by compilation of the list, and refers to the
generation of a medium for producing the required
number of copies (by stencil, offset, etc.) The information included at this point will depend on the purpose
of the list involved. Lists destined for accounts or
other administrative staff will probably contain brief
indentifying bibliographical elements and some degree of administrative information. Those lists
intended for wider distribution, such as new accession lists, abstract bulletins and subject reading lists,
will have varying degrees of fullness in their bibliographical descriptions and may include annotations.

A considerable amount of work is put in by library
staff involved, both in compiling and checking the
information presented. This is a good example of
one form fulfilling two functions, those of recording
and reporting, by a variance in usage. One copy is
filed, as a record of the listing procedure, others
are distributed to interested persons, and sometimes
to other libraries.

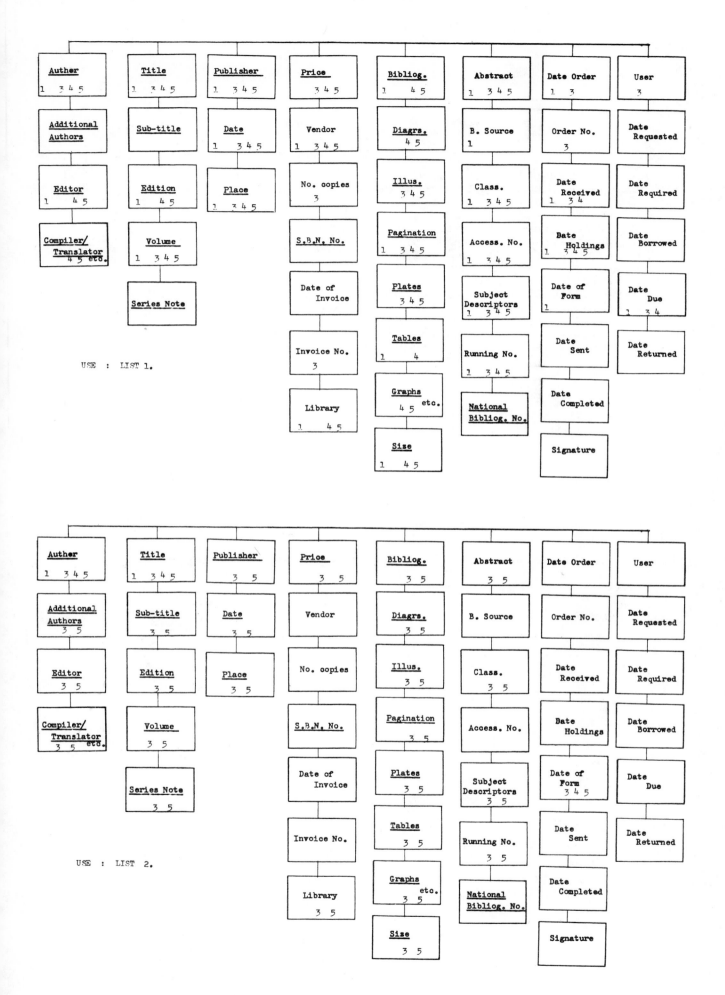

USE : LIST 1.

USE : LIST 2.

27

Use: Lend

Initiation can be by letter, but is more often done through the presentation of user and library book at the issue desk. In the first case it is necessary to know author, title and user, in the second, all inform- ation is supplied by the book/s and the user's registr- ation form (ticket, pocket, card, according to charging system in use). Authorisation takes place when the user first registers with the library, and is shewn by the registration form. In special libraries, employ- ment by the parent organisation is the usual qualifi- cation for membership, although arrangements can exist for lending to other persons/libraries. Public libraries require proof of residence in the area, or signature of a resident guarantor, and will keep regi- stration records.

Activation involves the giving of a date when the book is due for return and this is usually recorded in the book, on a date label or card, and the book then carries both its own bibliographical and processing informa- tion, and transaction details. Recording the loan of a book is the major activity in this procedure, and can be accomplished by noting details of book, user, and dates involved, again in a form appropriate to the charging system used.

Cancellation in this context covers the return and un- issue of books lent, and the relevant annotation or dis- carding of the loan records involved. Reporting of this procedure is not necessary, and if done at all involves statistical information on numbers of loans per day etc.

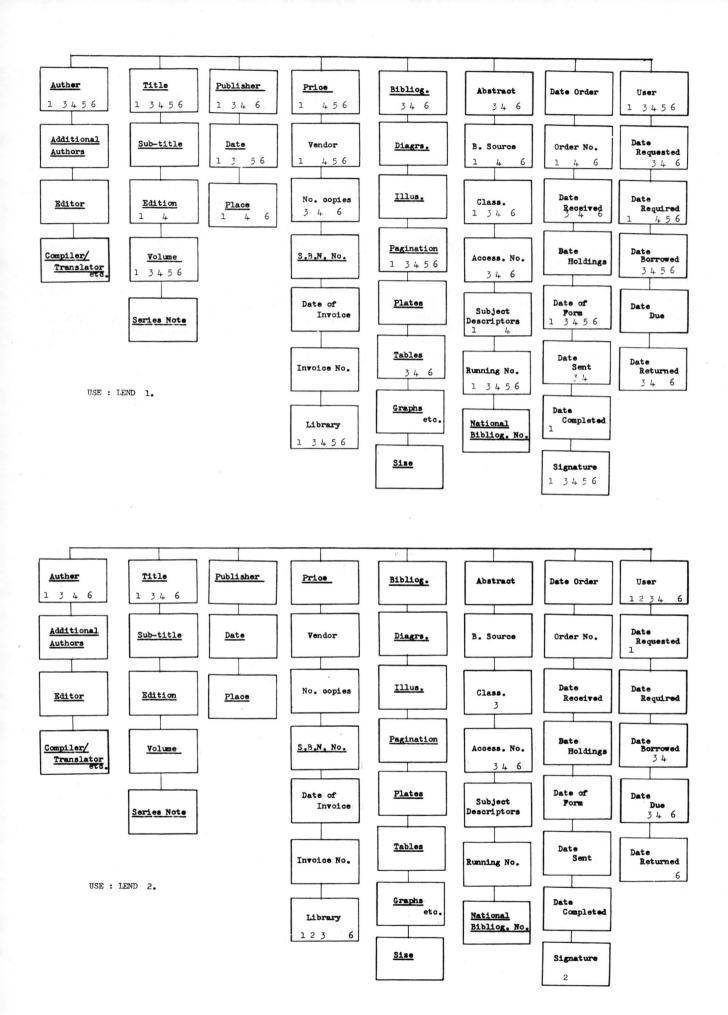

USE : LEND 1.

USE : LEND 2.

Use: Reserve

Most libraries provide for the reservation of required books not immediately available. Initiation is by reader's request card, or conversation, and can be triggered by the letters or telephone calls mentioned in the locating procedure. Activation will involve either the form already used in initiation or require the use of a similar one and recording is usually done by annotating and filing this record.

Reporting may be done by posting the original card to the user, or by telephoning or personal contact according to circumstances. This is usually done when the required book is again available for loan, or can inform on its non-availability through loss etc.

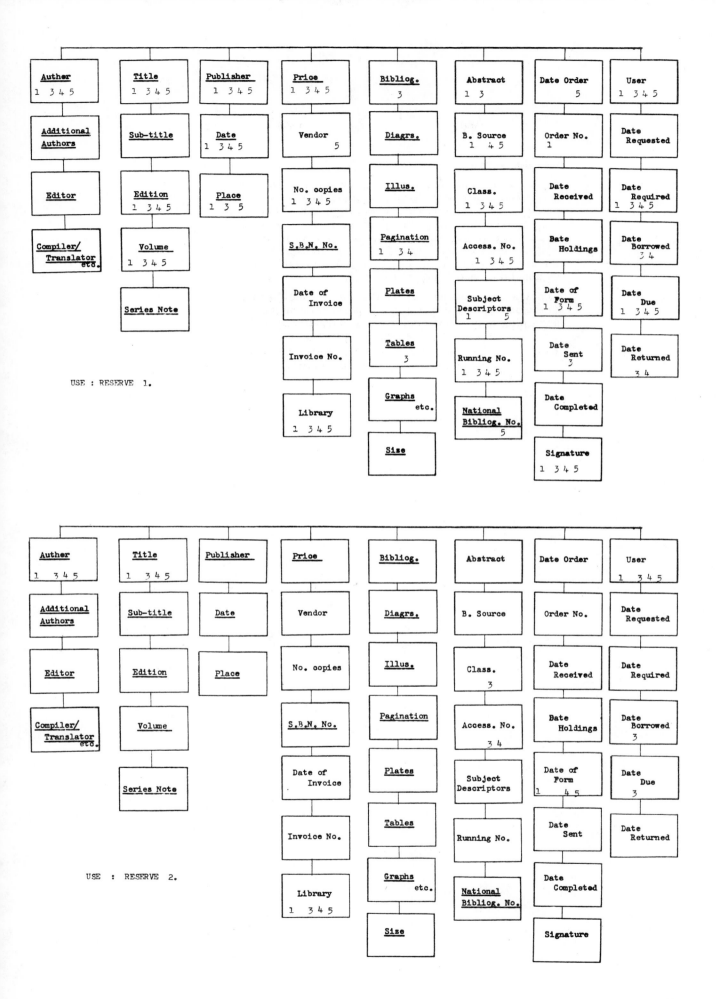

USE : RESERVE 1.

USE : RESERVE 2.

31

Use: Recall

When books are overdue, most libraries have a method for notifying the user and requesting the return or renewal of items in question. The simplest and possibly the most effective way to do this if circumstances permit is by telephone. There can be a whole range of overdue stationery involved, from the first polite postcard to the solicitor's letters of some public libraries.

Initiation is signalled by the loan records, activation involves the use of the appropriate form in the above mentioned range of pleas and commands. Recording is often done by annotating the loans record, and reporting is mainly concerned with accounting and legal aspects, and involves notifying other members of staff.

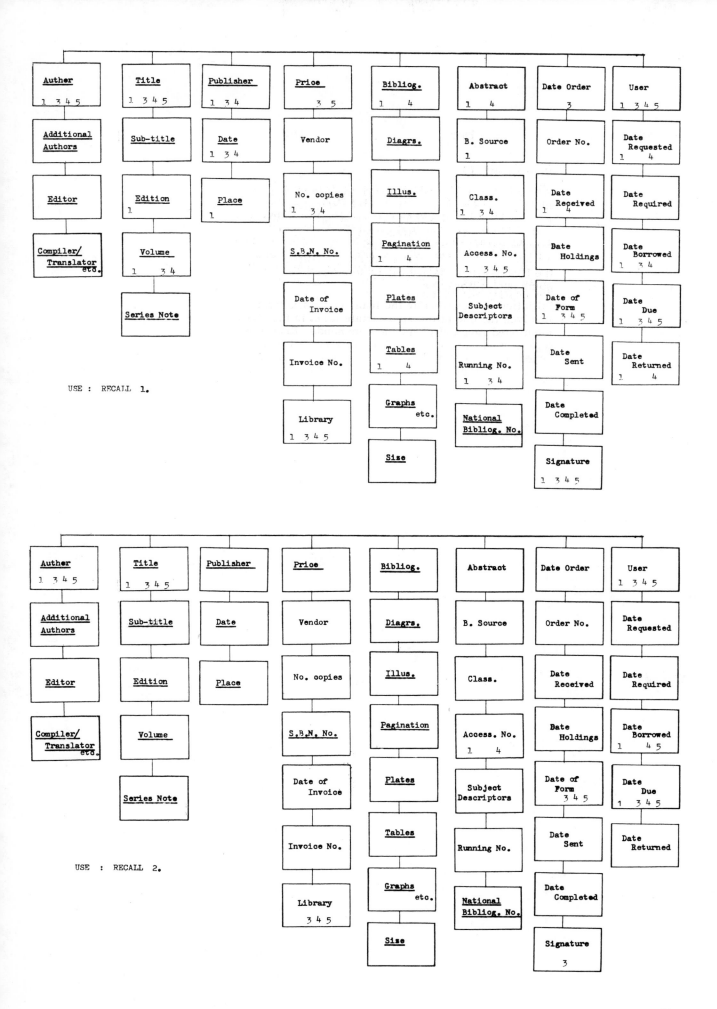

USE : RECALL 1.

USE : RECALL 2.

Use: Photocopy

The main uses for forms in this procedure are as statistical records for accounting purposes and in fulfilment of the requirements of the 1965 Copyright Act. The one form is often used for all five activities although others can be involved at the initiation stage (letter or telephone call) and activation may need a separate form where the photocopying is dealt with in another department, other forms may be necessary for costing and receipt purposes.

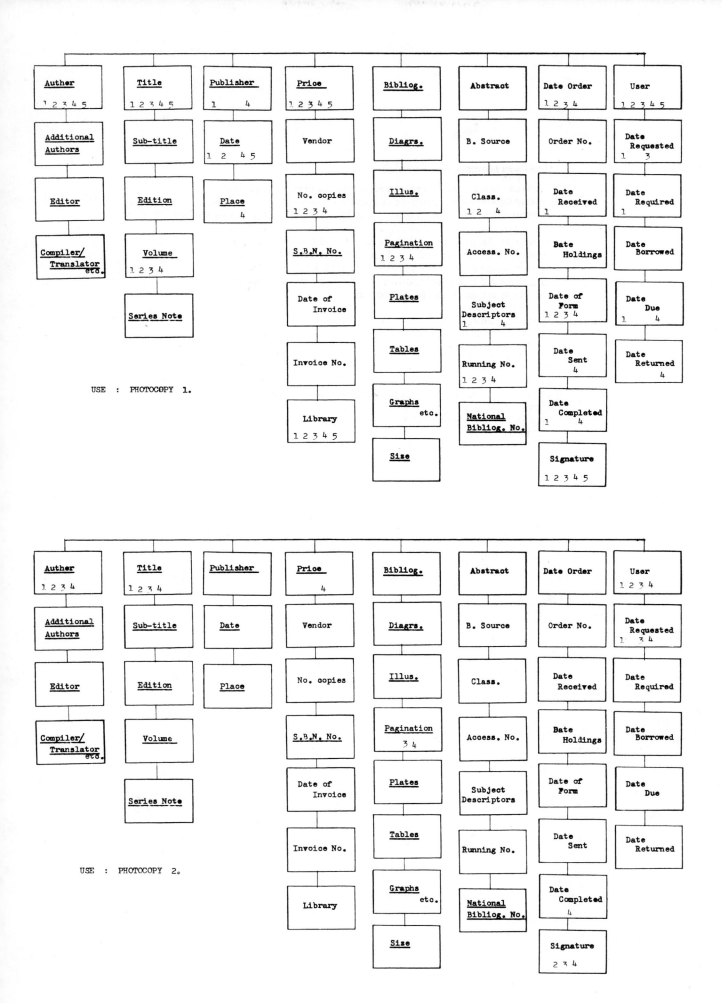

Auther 1 2 3 4 5	Title 1 2 3 4 5	Publisher 1 4	Price 1 2 3 4 5	Bibliog.	Abstract	Date Order 1 2 3 4	User 1 2 3 4 5
Additional Authors	Sub-title	Date 1 2 4 5	Vendor	Diagrs.	B. Source	Order No.	Date Requested 1 3
Editor	Edition	Place 4	No. copies 1 2 3 4	Illus.	Class. 1 2 4	Date Received 1	Date Required 1
Compiler/ Translator etc.	Volume 1 2 3 4		S.B.N. No.	Pagination 1 2 3 4	Access. No.	Bate Holdings	Date Borrowed
	Series Note		Date of Invoice	Plates	Subject Descriptors 1 4	Date of Form 1 2 3 4	Date Due 1 4
			Invoice No.	Tables	Running No. 1 2 3 4	Date Sent 4	Date Returned 4
			Library 1 2 3 4 5	Graphs etc.	National Bibliog. No.	Date Completed 1 4	
				Size		Signature 1 2 3 4 5	

USE : PHOTOCOPY 1.

Auther 1 2 3 4	Title 1 2 3 4	Publisher	Price 4	Bibliog.	Abstract	Date Order	User 1 2 3 4
Additional Authors	Sub-title	Date	Vendor	Diagrs.	B. Source	Order No.	Date Requested 1 3 4
Editor	Edition	Place	No. copies	Illus.	Class.	Date Received	Date Required
Compiler/ Translator etc.	Volume		S.B.N. No.	Pagination 3 4	Access. No.	Bate Holdings	Date Borrowed
	Series Note		Date of Invoice	Plates	Subject Descriptors	Date of Form	Date Due
			Invoice No.	Tables	Running No.	Date Sent	Date Returned
			Library	Graphs etc.	National Bibliog. No.	Date Completed 4	
				Size		Signature 2 3 4	

USE : PHOTOCOPY 2.

35

Use: Inter-Library Loans

The forms used in this procedure are mainly those dictated by outside organisations, such as NLL and the Regional Bureaux. The consensus diagrams, however, refer to forms generated internally to deal with the activities involved in both borrowing and lending through other libraries. For instance, a user's request may initiate the procedure, some libraries on the fringe of the inter-lending system request items on their own stationery, and many libraries keep records of their requests. Cancellation here refers to the return of a borrowed item, with connotations of post back and un-issue.

The optimal schematic is, as are all the optimal diagrams, based on the minimum information content necessary to each stage of the procedure. Therefore, although we present an optimal content for activation of this procedure, we are not trying to introduce a new inter-library loans form, only to establish basic information requirements in line with our procedural approach. We have not taken into consideration any local administrative constraints of the bureaux.

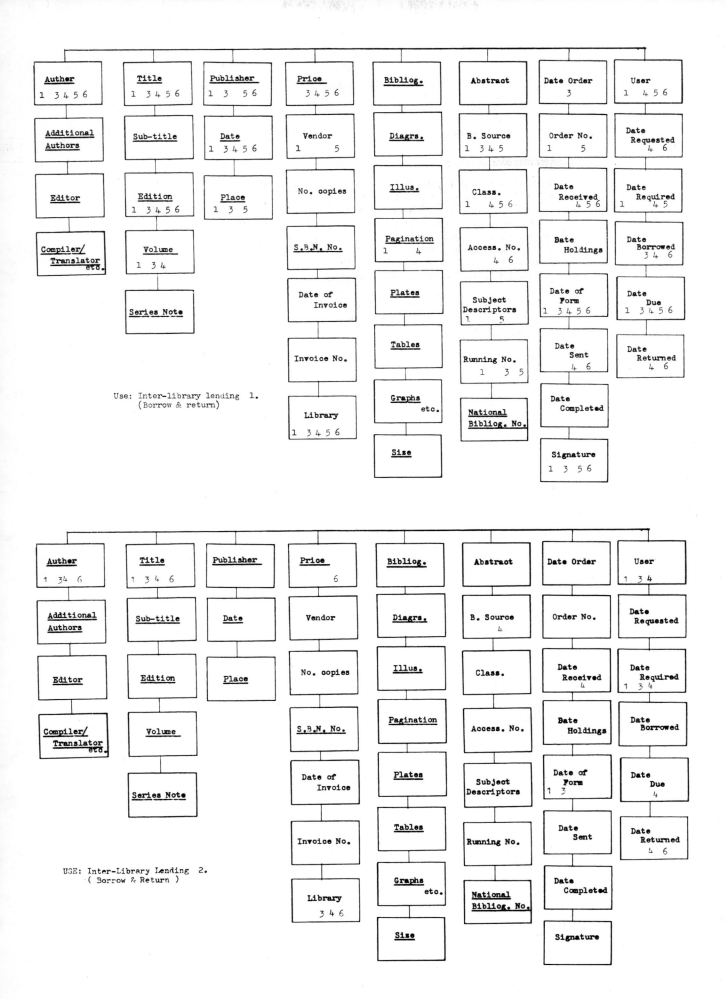

Auther 1 3456	Title 1 3 456	Publisher 1 3 56	Price 3456	Bibliog.	Abstract	Date Order 3	User 1 456
Additional Authors	Sub-title	Date 1 3456	Vendor 1 5	Diagrs.	B. Source 1 345	Order No. 1 5	Date Requested 4 6
Editor	Edition 1 3456	Place 1 3 5	No. copies	Illus.	Class. 1 456	Date Received 456	Date Required 1 45
Compiler/ Translator etc.	Volume 1 34		S.B.N. No.	Pagination 1 4	Access. No. 46	Bate Holdings	Date Borrowed 3 46
	Series Note		Date of Invoice	Plates	Subject Descriptors 1 5	Date of Form 1 3456	Date Due 1 3456
			Invoice No.	Tables	Running No. 1 3 5	Date Sent 46	Date Returned 46
			Library 1 3456	Graphs etc.	National Bibliog. No.	Date Completed	
				Size		Signature 1 3 56	

Use: Inter-library lending 1.
(Borrow & return)

Auther 1 34 6	Title 1 346	Publisher	Price 6	Bibliog.	Abstract	Date Order	User 1 34
Additional Authors	Sub-title	Date	Vendor	Diagrs.	B. Source 4	Order No.	Date Requested
Editor	Edition	Place	No. copies	Illus.	Class.	Date Received 4	Date Required 1 34
Compiler/ Translator etc.	Volume		S.B.N. No.	Pagination	Access. No.	Bate Holdings	Date Borrowed
	Series Note		Date of Invoice	Plates	Subject Descriptors	Date of Form 1 3	Date Due 4
			Invoice No.	Tables	Running No.	Date Sent	Date Returned 4 6
			Library 3 46	Graphs etc.	National Bibliog. No.	Date Completed	
				Size		Signature	

USE: Inter-Library Lending 2.
(Borrow & Return)

37

Maintenance: Bind

Forms involved in this procedure may well be those already generated in previous ones such as catalogue cards, book cards. Initiation is usually by the book itself, initiation by forms being more often restricted to periodicals. Activation can be by a list of items involved, one copy sent to the binder and the other filed as record of the action, and annotated, as the order form is often annotated, on the receipt of the items.

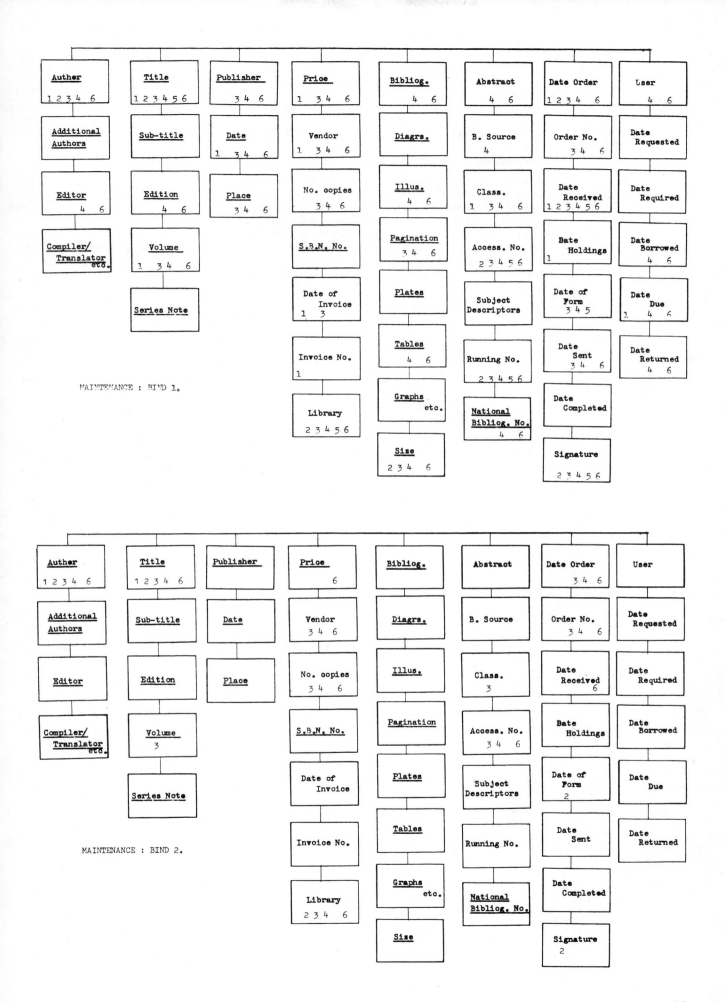

Auther	Title	Publisher	Price	Bibliog.	Abstract	Date Order	User
1 2 3 4 6	1 2 3 4 5 6	3 4 6	1 3 4 6	4 6	4 6	1 2 3 4 6	4 6

Additional Authors
Sub-title
Date   1 3 4 6
Vendor   1 3 4 6
Diagrs.
B. Source   4
Order No.   3 4 6
Date Requested

Editor   4 6
Edition   4 6
Place   3 4 6
No. copies   3 4 6
Illus.   4 6
Class.   1 3 4 6
Date Received   1 2 3 4 5 6
Date Required

Compiler/ Translator etc.
Volume   1 3 4 6
S.B.N. No.
Pagination   3 4 6
Access. No.   2 3 4 5 6
Bate Holdings   1
Date Borrowed   4 6

Series Note
Date of Invoice   1 3
Plates
Subject Descriptors
Date of Form   3 4 5
Date Due   1 4 6

Invoice No.   1
Tables   4 6
Running No.   2 3 4 5 6
Date Sent   3 4 6
Date Returned   4 6

Library   2 3 4 5 6
Graphs etc.
National Bibliog. No.   4 6
Date Completed

Size   2 3 4 6
Signature   2 3 4 5 6

MAINTENANCE : BIND 1.

Auther	Title	Publisher	Price	Bibliog.	Abstract	Date Order	User
1 2 3 4 6	1 2 3 4 6		6			3 4 6	

Additional Authors
Sub-title
Date
Vendor   3 4 6
Diagrs.
B. Source
Order No.   3 4 6
Date Requested

Editor
Edition
Place
No. copies   3 4 6
Illus.
Class.   3
Date Received   6
Date Required

Compiler/ Translator etc.
Volume   3
S.B.N. No.
Pagination
Access. No.   3 4 6
Bate Holdings
Date Borrowed

Series Note
Date of Invoice
Plates
Subject Descriptors
Date of Form   2
Date Due

Invoice No.
Tables
Running No.
Date Sent
Date Returned

Library   2 3 4 6
Graphs etc.
National Bibliog. No.
Date Completed

Size
Signature   2

MAINTENANCE : BIND 2.

Maintenance: Replace

This procedure can be triggered either by a decision
from the initiation of the binding one (if a book is
too badly damaged to be worth rebinding, and is in
print and important enough to replace) or by the loss
of a book. Previous records are often annotated, and
the form which activates replacement is absorbed
into the ordering procedure and the whole cycle
restarted.

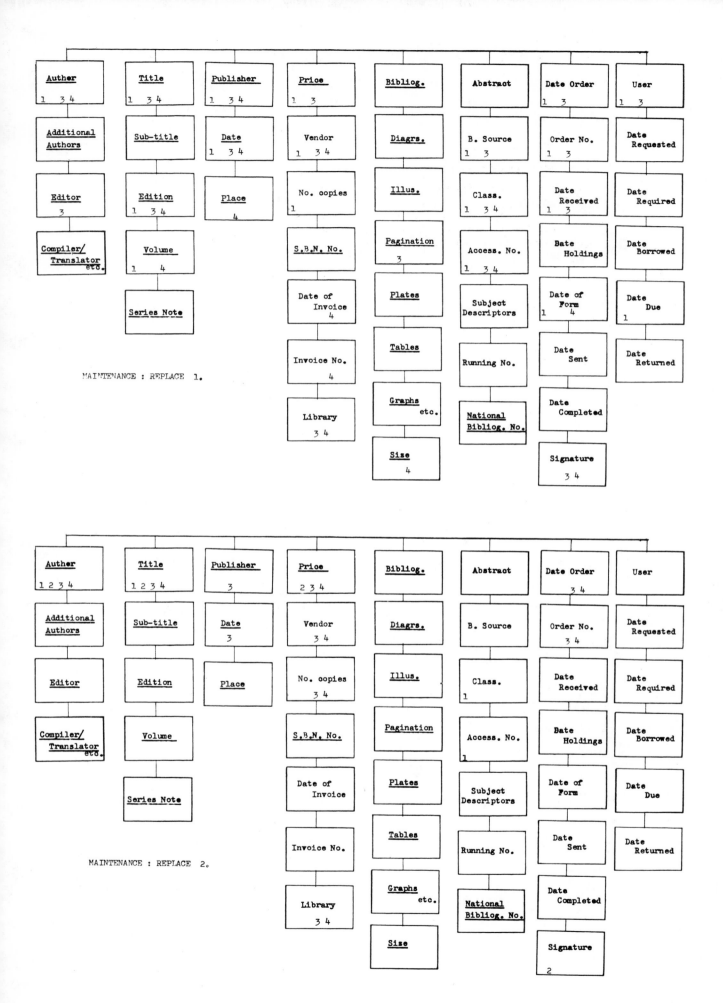

MAINTENANCE : REPLACE 1.

MAINTENANCE : REPLACE 2.

41

Maintenance: Discard

Again, this procedure is closely related to the others in this sub-system, and usually requires annotation of previous records. All records are generated and used by library staff for the replace and discard (withdraw) procedures, while the binding procedure involves a library supplier, the binder.

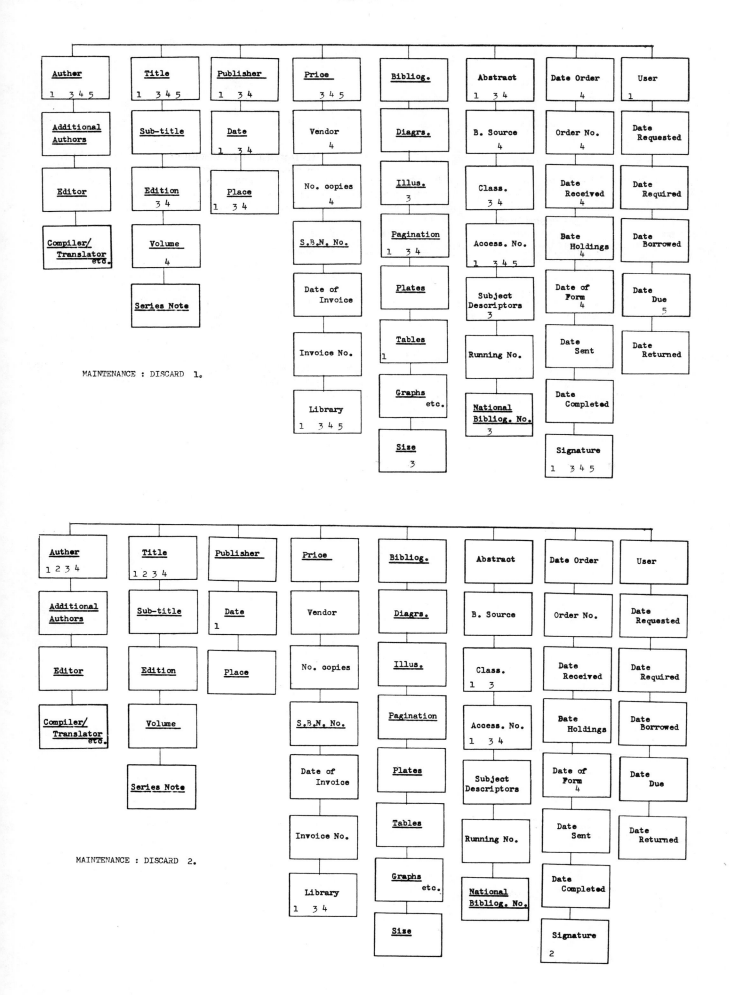

Auther	Title	Publisher	Price	Bibliog.	Abstract	Date Order	User
1 3 4 5	1 3 4 5	1 3 4	3 4 5		1 3 4	4	1
Additional Authors	Sub-title	Date	Vendor	Diagrs.	B. Source	Order No.	Date Requested
		1 3 4	4		4	4	
Editor	Edition	Place	No. copies	Illus.	Class.	Date Received	Date Required
	3 4	1 3 4	4	3	3 4	4	
Compiler/ Translator etc.	Volume		S.B.N. No.	Pagination	Access. No.	Bate Holdings	Date Borrowed
	4			1 3 4	1 3 4 5	4	
	Series Note		Date of Invoice	Plates	Subject Descriptors	Date of Form	Date Due
					3	4	5
			Invoice No.	Tables	Running No.	Date Sent	Date Returned
				1			
			Library	Graphs etc.	National Bibliog. No.	Date Completed	
			1 3 4 5		3		
				Sise		Signature	
				3		1 3 4 5	

MAINTENANCE : DISCARD 1.

Auther	Title	Publisher	Price	Bibliog.	Abstract	Date Order	User
1 2 3 4	1 2 3 4						
Additional Authors	Sub-title	Date	Vendor	Diagrs.	B. Source	Order No.	Date Requested
		1					
Editor	Edition	Place	No. copies	Illus.	Class.	Date Received	Date Required
					1 3		
Compiler/ Translator etc.	Volume		S.B.N. No.	Pagination	Access. No.	Bate Holdings	Date Borrowed
					1 3 4		
	Series Note		Date of Invoice	Plates	Subject Descriptors	Date of Form	Date Due
						4	
			Invoice No.	Tables	Running No.	Date Sent	Date Returned
			Library	Graphs etc.	National Bibliog. No.	Date Completed	
			1 3 4				
				Sise		Signature	
						2	

MAINTENANCE : DISCARD 2.

43

Processing: Catalogue

Forms are used in the same way in this procedure as in others and activities applicable are initiation (by the book itself), activation (copy for the production of the catalogue entry), and recording (by filing the entries so produced). Authorisation is shewn in some cases by the checking of copy and the addition of a signature or initials of the senior cataloguer.

Lacking general agreement on functions and content of the catalogue, and until more is known about the users' present and possibly desired approaches, we here present twelve schematic diagrams. Each one details those elements present in the catalogue entries of the libraries studied. As every book and every catalogue present different problems, these diagrams are based on discussions with the senior cataloguers of each library on their respective catalogue rules and practice. We show only those elements present in the 'record' activity, as this determines bibliographical information necessary for the other records involved, and have not included possible production requirements such as date, initials, numbers of cards etc. The presence of an element is indicated with an X.

Until catalogue functions have been more fully investigated, it would seem that the BNB/MARC communication record offers a significant amount of the required information. However, our diagrams show present information contents of catalogue entries only and we do not venture to prescribe an optimal set of elements as we have in other procedures. Should a library be unable to accept or adapt the BNB/MARC information to its own needs, then it must consider continuing to produce its own locally evolved records, or moving towards eventual compatibility with BNB/MARC entries.

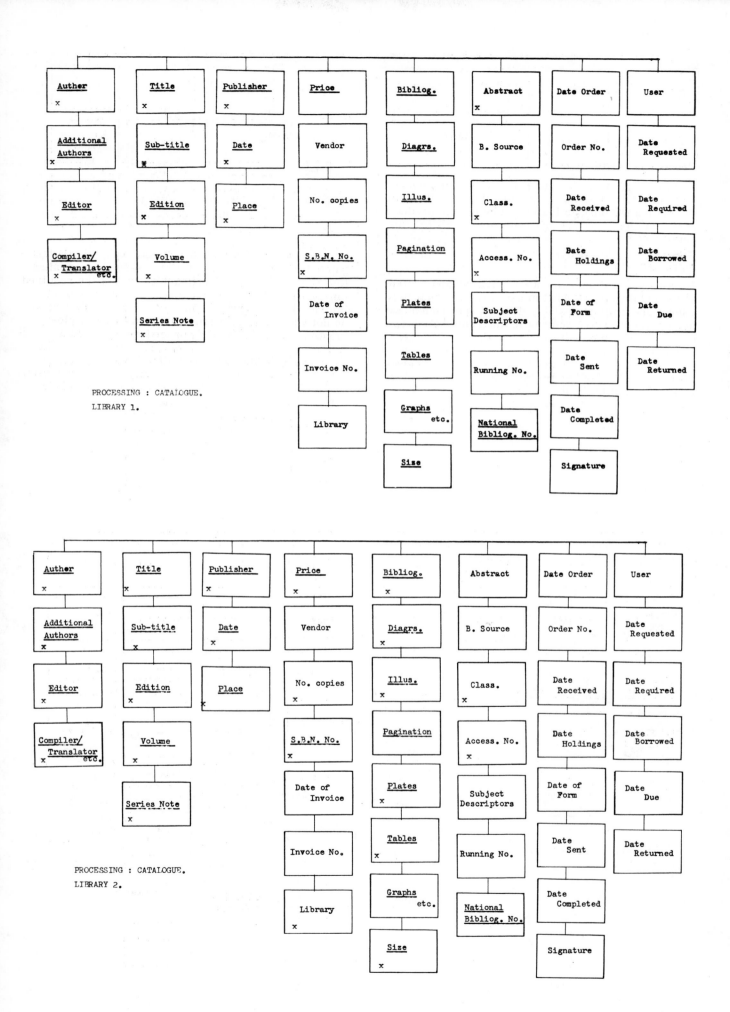

PROCESSING : CATALOGUE.
LIBRARY 1.

PROCESSING : CATALOGUE.
LIBRARY 2.

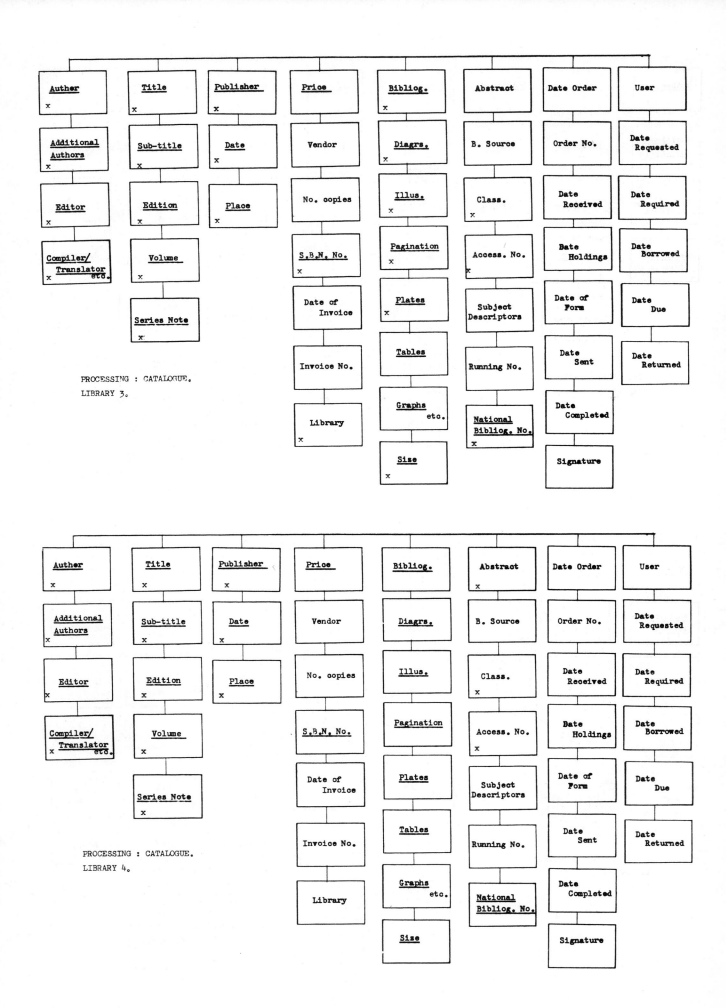

PROCESSING : CATALOGUE.
LIBRARY 3.

PROCESSING : CATALOGUE.
LIBRARY 4.

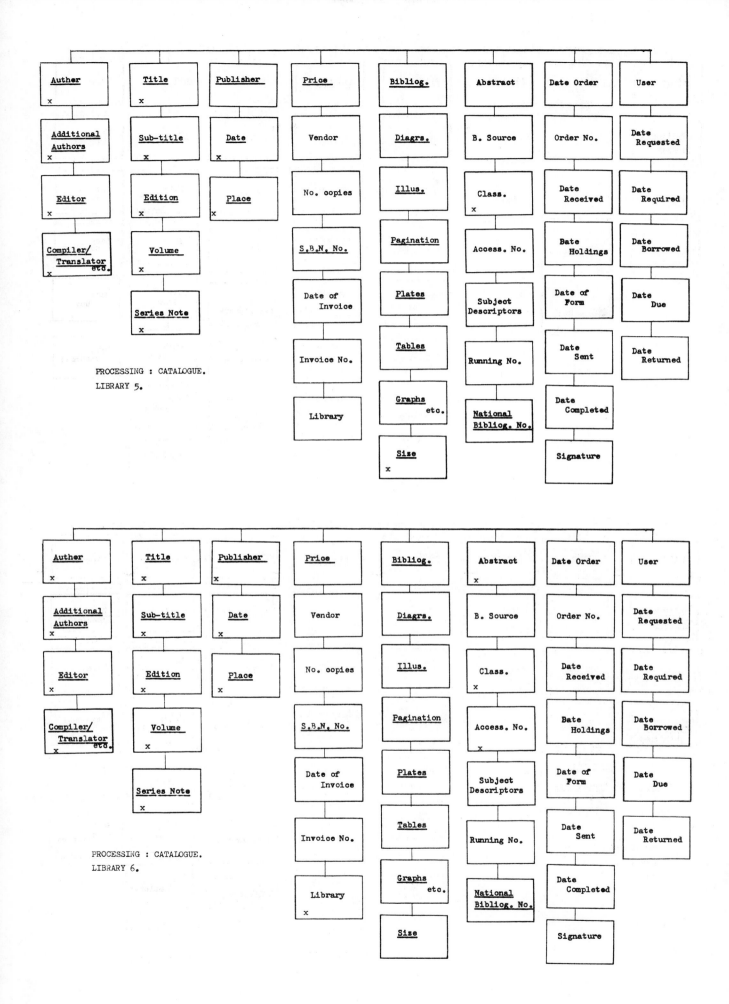

PROCESSING : CATALOGUE.
LIBRARY 5.

PROCESSING : CATALOGUE.
LIBRARY 6.

47

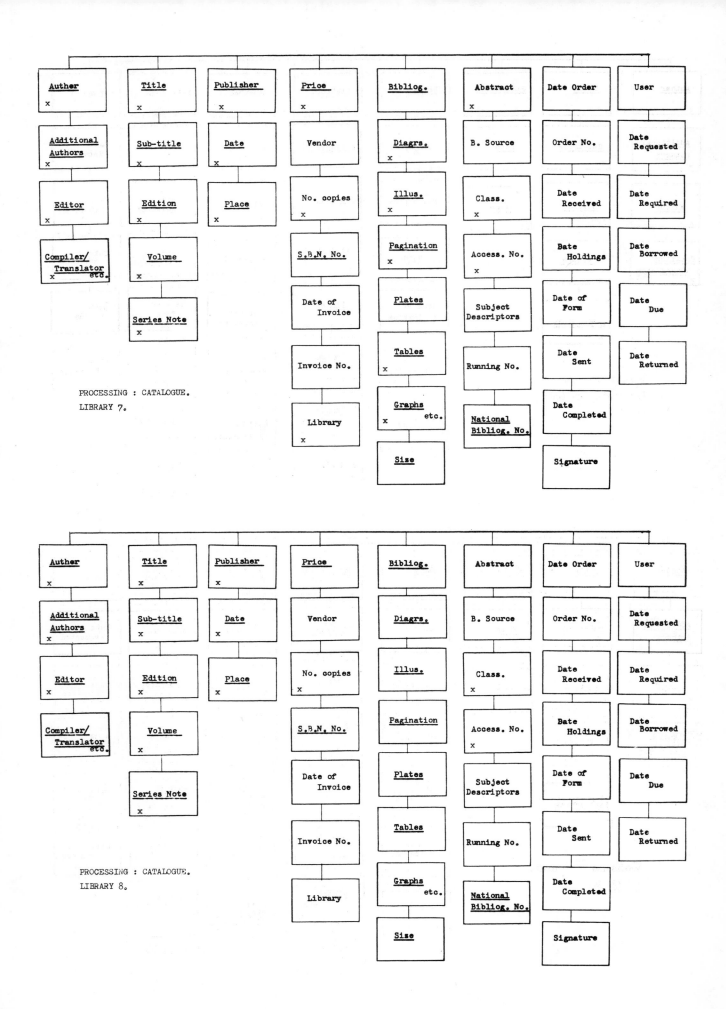

PROCESSING : CATALOGUE.
LIBRARY 7.

PROCESSING : CATALOGUE.
LIBRARY 8.

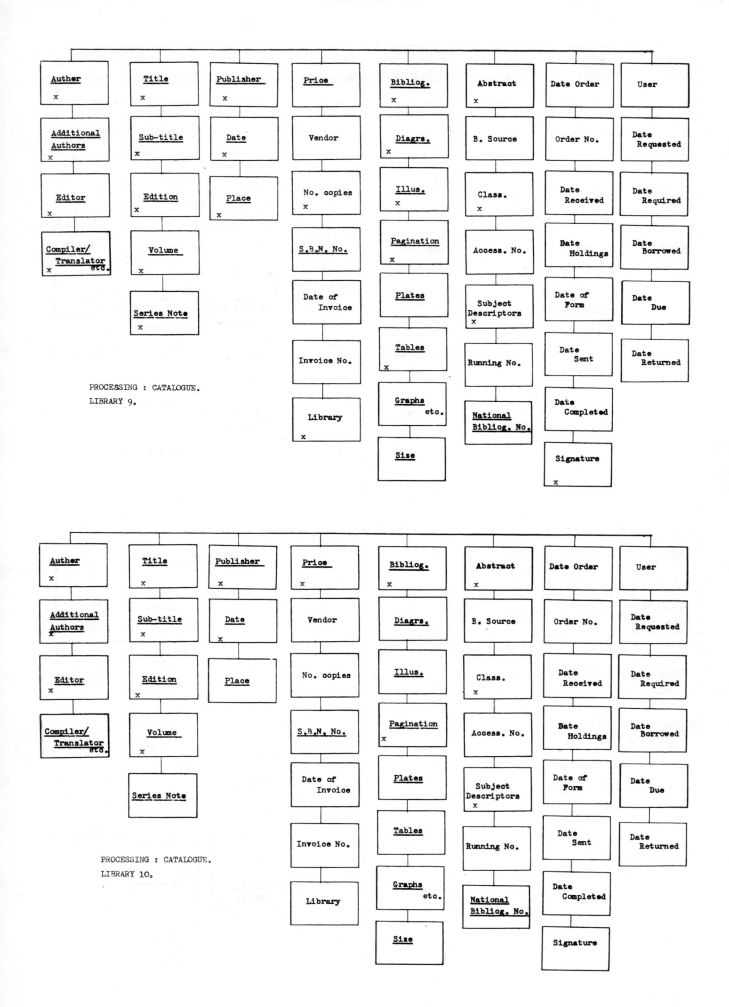

PROCESSING : CATALOGUE.
LIBRARY 9.

PROCESSING : CATALOGUE.
LIBRARY 10.

49

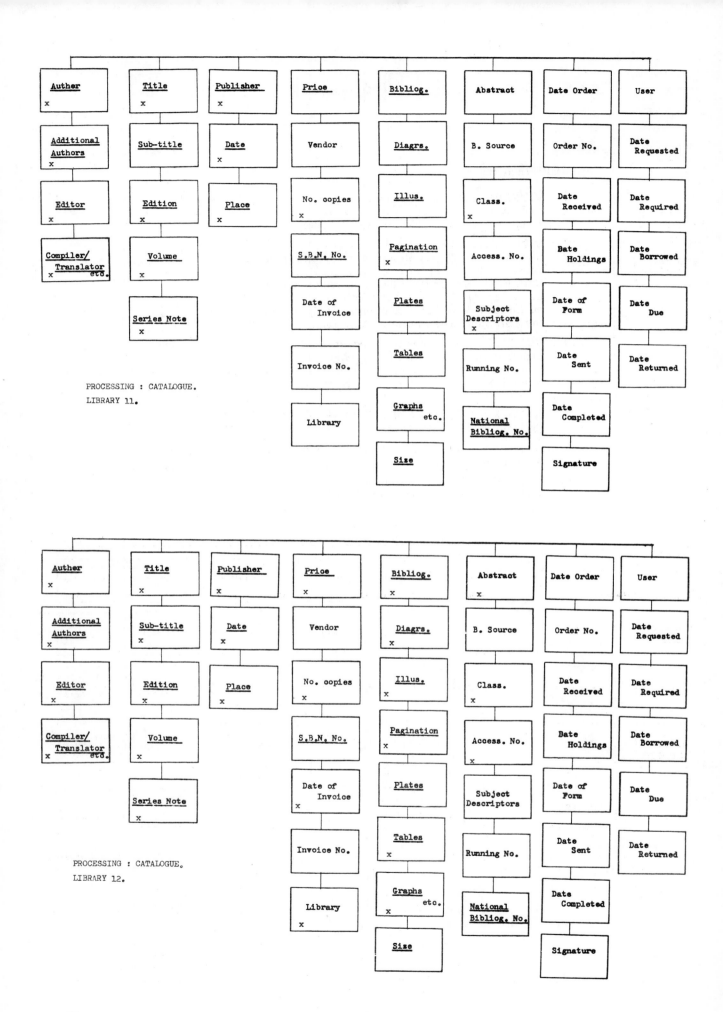

PROCESSING : CATALOGUE.
LIBRARY 11.

PROCESSING : CATALOGUE.
LIBRARY 12.

50

REFERENCES

1. VICKERY, B. C. Bibliographic description, arrangement, and retrieval. *Journal of Documentation,* vol. 24, No. 1, p 1-15, March 1968.

2. CURRAN, Ann *and* AVRAM, Henriette D. The identification of data elements in bibliographic records. Final Report of the Special Project on Data Elements for the Subcommittee on Machine Input Records (SC-2) of the Sectional Committee on Library Work and Documentation (Z-39) of the USA Standards Institute. May 1967.

3. HUNT, C. J. The computer production of catalogues of old books. *In Organisation and handling of bibliographic records by computer* edited by Nigel S. M. Cox and Michael W. Grose. Oriel Press. 1967.

4. GOLDSTEIN, K. Der Aufbau des Organismus. English translation: *'The Organism.'* 1939

5. LEVI-STRAUSS, Claude. Structural anthropology. Allen Lane Press, 1968.

6. KNOX, F. M. The knox standard guide to the design and control of business forms. McGraw Hill, 1965.

7. GROSE, M. W. *and* JONES, B. The Newcastle University Library order system. *In Organisation and handling of bibliographic records by computer.* Op. cit.